Leading Lady

CORETTA SCOTT KING

By Jill C. Wheeler

Published by Abdo & Daughters, 6535 Cecilia Circle, Edina, Minnesota 55439.

Library bound edition distributed by Rockbottom Books, Pentagon Tower, P.O. Box 36036, Minneapolis, Minnesota 55435.

Printed in the United States.

Cover Photo: Archive Photo's
Inside Photos: UPI Bettmann

Edited by Rosemary Wallner

LIBRARY OF CONGRESS CATALOGING-IN-PUBLICATION DATA

Wheeler, Jill C., 1964-
    Coretta Scott King / written by Jill C. Wheeler.
        p. cm. — (Leading Ladies)
    Summary: A biography of Coretta King, who worked side by side with her husband spreading a message of peace, love, and equality, and achieving those by nonviolent means.
    ISBN 1-56239-116-X
    1. King, Coretta Scott, 1927- --Juvenile literature. 2. King, Martin Luther, Jr., 1929-1968 -- Juvenile literature. 3. Afro-Americans --Biography--Juvenile literature. 4. Civil rights workers -- United States -- Biography -- Juvenile literature. [1. King, Coretta Scott, 1927- . 2. Civil rights workers. 3. Afro-Americans-Biography] I. Title. II. Series.
E185.97.K47W44   1992   323'.092--dc20   92-16677
                                                    [B]

International Standard	**Library of Congress**
Book Number:	**Catalog Card Number:**
1-56239-116-X	92-16677

TABLE OF CONTENTS

Former President Reagan signs a bill establishing a legal holiday in honor of slain civil rights leader, Dr. Martin Luther King, Jr., as his widow, Coretta Scott King, looks on during a ceremony in the Rose Garden.

A DREAM REALIZED

November 2, 1983, found Coretta Scott King very excited. President Ronald Reagan had invited her to the Rose Garden at the White House in Washington, D.C., for a special ceremony. Reagan was going to sign a law declaring a national holiday in honor of King's husband, the late Rev. Dr. Martin Luther King, Jr.

The ceremony marked the realization of a dream Coretta had harbored for nearly fifteen years. Her husband became the only American besides George Washington to be recognized with a national holiday. The holiday also reminded people of the U.S. Civil Rights Movement of the 1950s and 60s. People in the movement wanted all Americans treated equally, no matter what their skin color.

"Martin Luther King, Jr., and his spirit live within all of us," Coretta said during the ceremony. "Thank God for the blessing of his life and his leadership and his commitment. May we make ourselves worthy to carry on his dream."

Dr. King had shared his dream with a nation - a dream of equality and peace. He and Coretta had decided long before that they did not want their children to endure the hardships they had faced.

Together, they were able to make life better for millions of black Americans.

SEPARATE AND UNEQUAL

Coretta Scott learned at a young age that many people treated their fellow Americans differently because of their skin color. In the 1930s and 40s, she and her brother, Obie, and sister, Edythe, could not attend the same schools as white children. Their school was not as nice as the white children's school, and they had only two teachers for all six grades. The Scott children, like other black children, walked several miles to get to school. The white children in their home of Perry County, Alabama, rode a bus to school.

Life was very different for black and white people when King was growing up. Black people had separate schools, churches and restaurants. Blacks had to enter public buildings through the back door while whites could enter through the front door. When blacks and whites ate at the same lunch counters, the waitresses served blacks last. Blacks even had to use different drinking fountains, bathrooms and elevators than white people. This practice of separating blacks and whites is called segregation.

Segregated drinking fountain.

Police had the right to arrest blacks and jail them if they tried to go into white schools and restaurants. Some blacks broke segregation rules and angry whites beat or killed them. Many blacks obeyed the rules simply because they did not want to go to jail or die.

King's father, Obadiah Scott, vowed his family would have a good life in spite of these rules. He worked very hard to run the family farm, which had been in his family for three generations. He was the first black man in his community to own a truck. He bought a sawmill and operated a taxi service, as well as a filling station and grocery store.

Obadiah's success made many white men angry. They were afraid Obadiah would take work away from them, and some of them tried to hurt him. Once, a white police officer hit Obadiah. Another time, his sawmill mysteriously burned to the ground.

King quickly learned how difficult it was for blacks to stand up for their rights against whites. She, Obie and Edythe feared that white people might kill their father because he had tried to make a better life for his family.

STRUGGLING FOR AN
EDUCATION

King thought it was unfair that some white people treated
black people differently. She wanted to do something about
it. She decided the best way she could help black people
was to get a good education. Her mother, Bernice, who had
only a fourth-grade education, agreed. Bernice told her
daughters they would go to college even if they only had
one dress to wear.

Getting an education meant many sacrifices for King and
her family. The only high school that would take black students was ten miles away in Marion, Alabama. At first,
King lived in Marion and went home on weekends. Later,
her father converted one of his lumber trucks into a bus.
Her mother drove the bus forty miles each day to take her
children to Lincoln Missionary School and bring them
back home.

At Lincoln, King excelled in her studies. Her beautiful singing voice earned her soloist honors for the Lincoln choir
and in school musical productions. She graduated at the top
of her class and received a scholarship to Antioch College
in Yellow Springs, Ohio. She decided to earn a degree in
elementary education and take as many music courses as
she could.

*Coretta Scott posed with her classmates at Antioch College in Yellow Springs, Ohio
where she majored in music and elementary education.*

Eventually the time came for King to student teach. It shocked her to discover the local public school would not let her student teach because she was black. She asked the college officials to help her, but they said they could not. King had to settle for doing her student teaching at the private school operated by the college.

This experience spurred King to action. She joined the college's Race Relations Committee and other organizations dedicated to improving rights for black people. She wanted to improve conditions for future black students at Antioch. "I am a Negro and I'm going to be a Negro the rest of my life," she said. "I just can't let this kind of thing get me down."

As her graduation approached in June 1951, King considered what to do for a career. Many people told her she could be a concert singer. She took their advice and applied to the New England Conservatory of Music in Boston, Massachusetts. The school accepted her, and she won a grant to cover the cost of her tuition.

In Boston, King discovered it was difficult to pay all of her bills even though her grant covered tuition. She found a room in the home of a wealthy woman and arranged to clean part of the house in exchange for her rent. Still, for several days she lived on crackers, peanut butter and fruit. At one point, she had only fifteen cents.

Coretta discovered, upon meeting Martin Luther King, Jr., that she found his ideas about a better world were much like hers.

Finally, King found a job as a file clerk at a mail order firm. She paid for food and rent and continued her music studies. Her goal was to be a concert singer.

MEETING MARTIN LUTHER KING, JR.

While living in Boston, a friend suggested King meet a young man who was studying for his doctorate at Boston University. The man, Martin Luther King, Jr., was a minister from Atlanta, Georgia. At first, King said she did not want to meet him. She thought ministers were too stuffy and boring.

At last, she said Martin Luther King could call her. His opening line was, "I am like Napoleon at Waterloo before your charms." His remark did not impress her. She said, "Why, that's absurd. You haven't seen me yet."

After Martin's call, Coretta decided to have lunch with him. At first, she thought he was too short. When she got to know him better she found his ideas about a better world were much like hers. She discovered she enjoyed his company. "The more I saw of him, the more I liked him," she said.

Martin had hinted at marriage ever since their first date, but Coretta hesitated to make a commitment. She wanted to be a singer, not a minister's wife. Could she trade a life of concerts, pretty gowns and curtain calls to be the wife of a Southern minister?

In the end, King decided Martin's goals were worth working for. Perhaps, she thought, a singing career wasn't the most important goal in her life. She accepted his proposal and they were married at her home in Alabama on June 18, 1953.

Martin and Coretta returned to Boston that fall to complete school. At graduation time, Martin had job offers from two Northern churches, two Southern churches and three schools. He and Coretta talked about their options and decided to accept the offer from the Dexter Avenue Baptist Church in Montgomery, Alabama. They believed they could do more to help black people if they lived in the South, even though it would be easier to live in the North.

The Kings moved to Montgomery in September 1954. Just over a year later, on December 1, 1955, something happened in Montgomery that changed the face of the nation.

PROTEST ON THE BUS

The buses in Montgomery had special rules for blacks and whites. The rules said black people had to sit at the back of the bus. They also said blacks had to give their seats to whites when the white seats were filled.

On December 1, a bus driver asked a black seamstress, Rosa Parks, to give her seat to a white man. Parks was very tired that day and she refused. The driver called a police officer and the officer arrested her.

The arrest triggered a wave of anger in the black community. Martin Luther King, Jr., decided to harness the anger to make the city change its bus rules. He did not believe in using violence to achieve change. Instead, he asked all black people to stop riding the bus. He knew most of the city's bus riders were black. Without them, the bus system would lose lots of money.

King did not know what she and Martin would do if the boycott was not a success. The day the boycott began, she anxiously watched the street outside their house. As the first bus drove past, she cried out in delight, "Darling, it's empty!"

Mrs. Rosa Parks' arrest on December 1, 1955 for sitting in a bus forward of white passengers, touched off the boycott of Montgomery, Alabama Negroes against the city bus lines.

All across Montgomery, the city's 50,000 blacks walked, took taxis or rode with friends to get to work. Some even used horses and mules, but no blacks rode the bus. Dr. King told city officials no blacks would ride the buses until the bus company made three changes.

First, he asked bus drivers to be courteous to black riders. Second, blacks wanted to be able to sit anywhere on the bus. They believed the first person who took a seat should be able to keep it, regardless of their color. Finally, they wanted the bus company to hire black drivers for routes that carried many black passengers.

The boycott made the city leaders and the bus company very angry. They were angry with Dr. King for leading the boycott, too. Some people called the King home to make threats.

Two months into the boycott, Coretta was at home with a friend and her two-month-old baby, Yolanda, when she heard a noise on the porch. She hurried to the back of the house where the baby was and heard an explosion. She realized someone had bombed their house.

Dr. King worried about the safety of his wife and daughter. Coretta's father suggested she and the baby move back with him for a while. She refused.

"I really wouldn't be happy if I did go," she said. "I would rather stay here with Martin."

Coretta's calm attitude after the bombing amazed many people. Later, she said she lost her fear of dying the day their house was bombed. She also believed, more than ever, that she and Martin had an important job to do.

A jury convicted Rosa Parks of violating the city's laws on the very day the bus boycott began. She appealed her case all the way to the U.S. Supreme Court. In November 1956, the Supreme Court said Montgomery's laws violated the U.S. Constitution and had to be changed. Martin and Coretta had won their first major victory.

A BRUSH WITH DEATH

King had grown up living with the fear of losing her father. Now, her fears were for the safety of Martin and her children, Yolanda and Martin Luther King III. Her fears materialized on September 20, 1958, when a mentally ill woman stabbed Dr. King in the chest with a letter opener. He was autographing books in New York City when the woman attacked him.

The letter opener had come to rest against Martin's heart. Had he sneezed or moved wrong, the opener would have killed him at once. King flew to New York as soon as she heard the news. She set up an office in the hospital where Dr. King was resting to conduct the business of the Civil Rights Movement. Even after her husband left the hospital, she continued to travel, deliver speeches and take care of details while he worked. Many people credit Coretta for holding the movement together during her husband's recovery.

"I have taken my responsibility as a wife and mother seriously, as I take my role of wife to the leading symbol of the Civil Rights struggle," King said. "I have tried to understand and fulfill these roles. I am aware of my personal limitations. At every point I have believed that the cause was most important, and I have been willing to make the necessary sacrifices."

Being the wife of Martin Luther King, Jr., meant making many sacrifices. Her husband often traveled, so the family had limited time together. Still, King made the most of their time together and did not complain when Dr. King was gone. "It pleases me greatly that Martin is admired," she said once. "So I don't mind sharing him as he shakes hands and signs autographs for his many admirers."

Martin Luther King, Jr., comforted by his wife in a Harlem hospital, after he was stabbed in the chest.

King also put her musical talents to work helping the Movement. She created a "Freedom Concert" of songs, poetry and readings that she performed around the nation. Once Dr. King was afraid he would not be able to pay his staff members. At the last minute, a $2,000 check came from one of Coretta's concerts and saved the day.

A CALL FROM THE PRESIDENT

In 1960, the Kings moved to Atlanta so Dr. King could serve the Ebenezer Baptist Church. His father and grandfather also had served that church. In January of the following year, Atlanta police sent Dr. King to jail for helping with a protest. At first, the Kings believed the jail sentence would be routine. However, they discovered a little-known law that gave authorities the right to send Martin to prison to do hard labor. Police put Martin in chains and transferred him to the prison in the middle of the night.

The transfer upset Coretta. The prison was four hours away, and she was afraid Martin would be hurt there. She also worried the prison guards would take away the reading and writing materials he used when he was in jail.

Martin Luther King, Jr., meeting with U.S. Senator, John F. Kennedy.

Then the phone rang. It was a call for King from a U.S. Senator named John F. Kennedy. "I just wanted you to know that I am concerned," Senator Kennedy told her. "We are going to do everything we can to help." The next day, Dr. King was released from prison.

Senator Kennedy went on to become President of the United States. He and Dr. King worked together on several Civil Rights projects, but it wasn't until April 1963 that Coretta talked with Kennedy again. Once more, police had put Dr. King in jail for his work to help blacks. This time, the police would not let him make even one phone call. King became very worried when she did not hear from her husband.

Friends urged her to contact President Kennedy for help. At first, King was unable to reach the president. Instead, she spoke with some members of his staff and his brother, U.S. Attorney General Robert Kennedy. Robert Kennedy learned Dr. King was safe but the police would not let him communicate with anyone.

The next day, the phone rang again. It was President John Kennedy to tell King that he had talked with the prison officials and Dr. King would call her soon. After his release, Martin told Coretta his treatment had mysteriously improved after a few days.

Seated with Mrs. King at the piano are her children (L to R) Yolanda, Bernice, Dexter and Martin Luther III, singing freedom songs.

Both believed it was because of the president's call. They were very sad later that year when an assassin shot and killed President Kennedy. Black Americans and the entire Civil Rights Movement had lost a friend in President Kennedy.

LIFE IN THE MOVEMENT

For another five years, the Kings continued their struggle to make the world a better place. Coretta traveled to Geneva, Switzerland, in 1962 to attend an international peace conference. Two years later, Dr. King received a Nobel Prize for Peace. At age thirty-five, he was the youngest person ever to receive the award.

Her husband's work sometimes made it difficult for King to raise her four children. In addition to Yolanda and Martin Luther King III, she had another son, Dexter, in 1961 and a daughter, Bernice, in 1963. When Dr. King was imprisoned, she had to explain to the children that their father was not a bad person because he was in jail. She also taught them that black people were good people – they were no different from others just because they had dark skin.

King's deep faith in God and her love for her children kept her going many times when bad things happened to her and Dr. King. "I want my children to be free of prejudice against others and at the same time maintain a pride in and identify with their race," she said.

She also spoke out about what the Civil Rights Movement demanded from its followers. "I believe very strongly that a person must dedicate himself to what he believes," she said. "When you decide to give yourself to a great cause, you must arrive at the point where no sacrifice is too great."

TRAGEDY IN MEMPHIS

In March 1968, Dr. King learned of a series of non-violent protests by the black garbage collectors of Memphis, Tennessee. He decided to visit Memphis to show his support for the movement. He also planned to begin a march in Memphis as part of his planned Poor People's Campaign. The campaign would call attention to the problems faced by poor people of all races.

On the evening of April 4, 1968, Dr. King was preparing for dinner. He stepped out on to the balcony of his motel room to speak with a staff member.

Suddenly a shot rang out and he crumpled to the floor, a bullet wound in his neck. He was dead within minutes.

One of Dr. King's staff members with him in Memphis was a young minister named Jesse Jackson. Jackson called Coretta to tell her someone had shot her husband. Coretta rushed to the airport to fly to Memphis. While waiting for her flight, Martin's personal secretary told Coretta the radio news report had said Martin was dead. Coretta quietly got into a friend's car for the drive back to her home.

In the aftermath of the shooting, Coretta presented a calm exterior to the world. As before, when her husband was stabbed, she cried in private, then composed herself for public appearances. When the plane carrying Dr. King's body arrived at the Atlanta airport, Coretta thought only of others. Seeing the many crying people who had gathered there she said, "They are the ones who need help now."

Dr. King's death sparked grief and anger across the nation. Riots broke out in more than sixty cities, and forty-three people died. Coretta feared the Civil Rights Movement would turn violent without Dr. King's leadership. He had always said he hoped people would not resort to violence if he were killed.

PICKING UP THE PIECES

Coretta quickly held a press conference urging people to continue protesting non-violently. She told reporters, "My husband told the children that if a man had nothing worth dying for, then he was not fit to live. He also said it's not how long you live but how well you live."

The day before Martin's funeral, Coretta went to Memphis to lead the Poor People's Campaign march her husband had planned. People were surprised she had the strength to lead the two-mile march. She also gave a speech.

"We must carry on," she told the crowd of 15,000 people. "This is the way he would have wanted it to have been. We are going to continue his work to make all people truly free and to make every person feel that he is a human being."

The following day was Dr. King's funeral at Ebenezer Baptist Church. It was the largest funeral ever held for a private citizen in the United States. One hundred and fifty thousand people attended. Among those in attendance was Jacqueline Kennedy , widow of President John Kennedy. After the funeral, Mrs. Kennedy embraced the new widow.

*Coretta Scott King comforts her youngest daughter, Bernice, 5, during funeral
services for her slain husband, Martin Luther King, Jr.,
at the Ebenezer Church, April 9, 1968.*

King knew Kennedy was one of the few people who could truly understand what she was going through.

King continued to carry on as she believed her husband would have wanted her to. She took his place at the speaking engagements he had arranged. Less than a month after he died, King led a thousand people in the Poor People's Campaign march to Washington, D.C. One month after that, she flew to California to comfort the widow of Robert Kennedy, who also had been assassinated.

King learned on the day of Robert Kennedy's funeral that police had captured James Earl Ray, a suspect in the murder of her husband. Ray later pleaded guilty to murdering Dr. King. King said she did not want Ray to receive the death penalty. Like her husband, she had learned to turn the other cheek.

KEEPING THE DREAM ALIVE

In the following years, King continued the struggle her husband had begun. She became the first woman ever to speak at St. Paul's Cathedral in London. She received an honorary degree from Boston University, where Martin had earned his doctorate.

Coretta Scott King addresses the 25th Anniversary of the march on Washington
before a crowd of 50,000. Mrs. King is surrounded by her children,
(L to R) Yolanda, Bernice, Martin Luther King III and Dexter.

She traveled to Italy, Jamaica and India spreading Dr. King's message of peace, love and equality. In the United States, she continued to speak and lead marches and peaceful demonstrations.

Today, King keeps busy as founding president and chief executive officer of The Martin Luther King, Jr. Center For Nonviolent Social Change. The Center has grown from a room in the basement of her home to a huge complex employing 63 people. Inside its walls, young people learn how to make a difference through nonviolent activism and social programs. Outside the center, King maintains a hectic schedule of speaking engagements and meetings. Many days, she is busy well past midnight, but she always finds time to spend with her children.

King said she believes American blacks have made progress, but much remains to be done. "A few decades ago skeptics scoffed at the idea of organ transplants and people walking on the moon," she said in a 1990 interview. "But if we work courageously and pray faithfully with a spirit of sacrifice, we can achieve further reforms which now seem unimaginable."